W9-AXS-815

INFORMATION EXPLORER

SUPER SMART INFORMATION STRATEGIES

SHARED CREATIONS: MAKING USE OF CREATIVE COMMONS

by Emily Puckett Rodgers and Kristin Fontichiaro

CHERRY LAKE PUBLISHING • ANN ARBOR, MICHIGAN

CHERRY LAKE Publishing

A NOTE TO PARENTS AND TEACHERS: Please remind your children how to stay safe online before they do the activities in this book.

A NOTE TO KIDS: Always remember your safety comes first!

Published in the United States of America
by Cherry Lake Publishing
Ann Arbor, Michigan
www.cherrylakepublishing.com

Content Adviser: Gail Dickinson, PhD, Associate Professor, Old Dominion University, Norfolk, Virginia

Photo Credits: Cover, ©NASA Goddard Photo and Video / http://www.flickr. / http://www.flickr.com / CC-B-2.0; page 4 ©woodleywonderworks0 / http://www.flickr. com / CC-BY-2.0; page 5, © MikeBlogs / http://www.flickr.com / CC-BY-SA-2.0; page 7, ©Skokie Northshore Sculpture Par / http://www.flickr.com / CC-BY--ND-2.0; page 10, ©racheocity / http://www.flickr.com / CC-BY--ND-2.0; page 11, George Washington, by Gilbert Stuart (Sterling and Francine Clark Art Institute); page 13, ©puuikibeach / http://www.flickr.com / CC-BY-2.0; page 15, ©net_efekt / http://www.flickr.com / CC-BY-2.0; page 16, ©Bhavna Sayana / http://www.flickr.com / CC-BY-2.0; page 17 ©cambodia4kidsorg / http://www. flickr.com / CC-BY-2.0; page 21, ©xoque / http://www.flickr.com / CC-BY-SA-2.0; page 23, This is a derivative of ©xoque / http://www.flickr.com / CC-BY-SA-2.0; page 24, U.S. Airforce Tech. Sgt. Andy Dunaway/Wikimedia Commons/Public Domain; page 27, This is a derivative of ©aussiegall / http://www.flickr.com / CC-BY-2.0; page 28, Clock designed by Luis Prado from The Noun Project, Flower from The Noun Project, Palm Tree designed by Jouko Luhola from The Noun Project, Laptop designed by Sam Ahmed from The Noun Project, Soccer designed by Derek Britton from The Noun Project, School Bus Stop collaboration by Edward Boatman, Shan Gao, Gene Lu, and Tina Ye.

Library of Congress Cataloging-in-Publication Data
Rodgers, Emily Puckett.
  Shared creations : making use of Creative Commons / by Emily Puckett Rodgers and Kristin Fontichiaro.
      pages cm. — (Information explorer)
  Includes bibliographical references and index.
    ISBN 978-1-62431-020-1 (lib. bdg.) — ISBN 978-1-62431-044-7 (pbk.) —
ISBN 978-1-62431-068-3 (e-book)
    1. Copyright—Juvenile literature. 2. Public domain (Copyright law)--Juvenile literature.
3. Copyright licenses—Juvenile literature. 4. Creative Commons (Organization)—Juvenile
literature. 5. Information commons—Juvenile literature. I. Fontichiaro, Kristin. II. Title.
    K1440.F66 2013   2012035760
    346.04'82—dc23

Cherry Lake Publishing would like to acknowledge the work of The Partnership for 21st Century Skills. Please visit www.21stcenturyskills.org for more information.

Printed in the United States of America
Corporate Graphics Inc.
January 2013
CLSP12

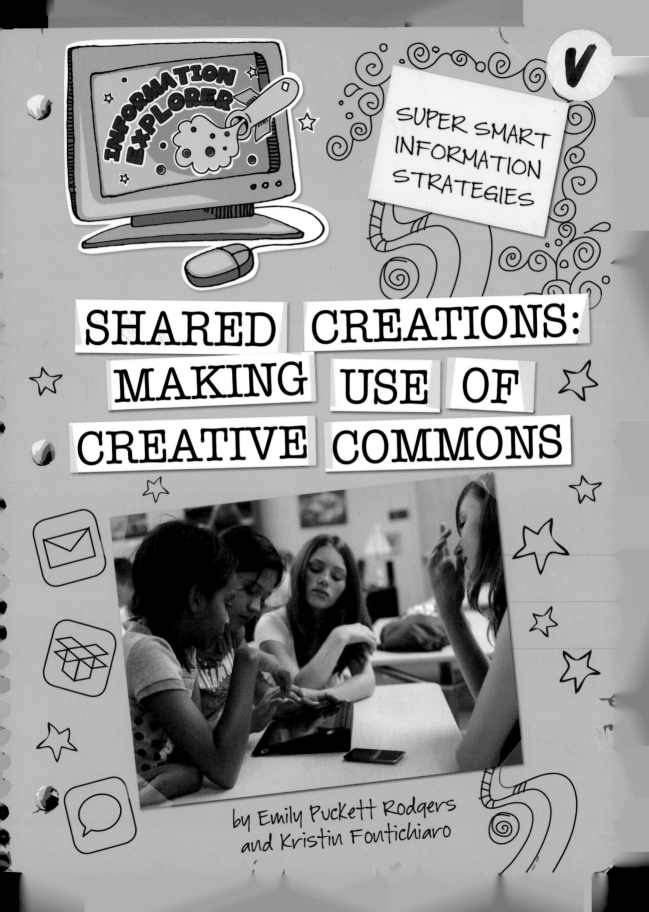

INFORMATION EXPLORER

SUPER SMART
INFORMATION
STRATEGIES

SHARED CREATIONS: MAKING USE OF CREATIVE COMMONS

by Emily Puckett Rodgers
and Kristin Fontichiaro

Table of Contents

CHAPTER ONE
What Is Copyright?

Make sure you give credit to the creators if you use other people's words or images in a project. This book does. Take a look at page 2, after the title page.

You've worked hard on a great slideshow presentation. It has plenty of pictures. When you post it to your class Web site, your teacher says, "This is good work, but you really shouldn't use other people's **copyrighted** materials in your slides." What does that mean?

Your teacher is reminding you that—oops!—you used other people's words, videos, audio recordings, or images in your project. Then you published their work with yours, without asking their permission.

You probably found the information in books, films, Web sites, or other sources. Though you may not have copied their works directly, you still need to give them credit.

What is copyright? You may have seen words like "copyright 2013" or "© 2013" in books, on CD sleeves, or in movie credits. Copyright means that the person or organization that created the work gets to decide how it is used. From the moment an article, picture, note, poster, podcast, or video is created, that work is automatically protected by U.S. and international copyright law. That gives the creators control over how their works are used by others. The same is

The copyright symbol lets you know that the words, music, images, or other creations are protected.

true for you—from the moment you create something, copyright law protects your work. Even if you find something online, it's still copyrighted unless it says otherwise. It never hurts to add "copyright 2013" to your work. But even without those words, someone's work is protected in the same way those movies or CDs are. Some people mail their work off to the Library of Congress, but this isn't necessary.

Copyright is actually a set of five rights. These rights let the creator of a work decide how others can use that work. Creators control who can:

1. make copies of their work, such as prints, photocopies, or electronic copies;
2. make any **derivatives**, which are new versions or adaptations of a work, whether using part of the work or all of it;
3. distribute copies of the work, such as in a bookstore or on a Web site;
4. display the work in public, for example, at an art gallery or on a Web site; and

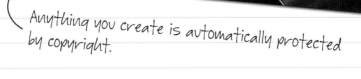

Anything you create is automatically protected by copyright.

5. publicly perform the work if the work is a play, piece of music, ballet, or anything else that can be performed by others.

A creative work is original writing, art, photographs, audio, images, music scores, song lyrics, or even the dance steps for a ballet company. All of those can be copyrighted. It doesn't matter whether a famous author like Rick Riordan creates it or whether you do. It's one of your rights as a world citizen.

Your works are copyrighted, but you cannot copy-right ideas. Imagine that Grace came up with a cool idea to thread beads through her shoelaces. Right now, it's just an *idea*. Because ideas cannot be copyrighted, any-one else can thread beads through *their* shoelaces and it's perfectly OK. However, if Grace took a photograph of those beads, the photo is automatically copyrighted. What about Grace's video demonstration, her project sketch, or her pamphlet of directions on how to thread beads through shoelaces? They are automatically copy-righted, too. All of these put the idea into what copyright experts call a **tangible format**—a documentation of the idea, written or recorded in Grace's unique way. It's Grace's expression (or version) of the idea that is hers to use and to give permission to others to use.

Tangible formats include photos, brochures, and other documentations of an idea.

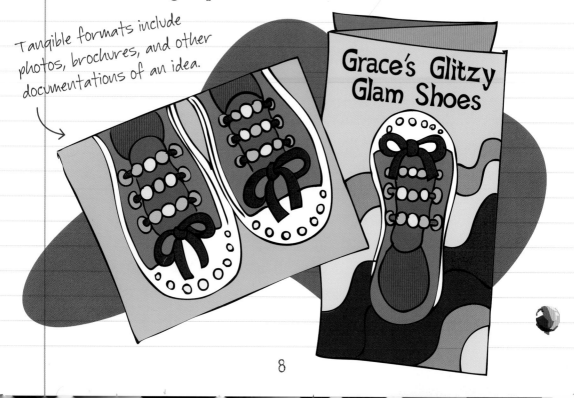

Grace's Glitzy Glam Shoes

TRY THIS!

Create some copyrighted work! Gather a group of friends. Give each person (and yourself) a blank piece of paper. Call out something for everyone to draw, such as your teacher, a tree, or a dog. After everyone has had a chance to draw, share everyone's drawings. They are all different! You cannot copyright an actual teacher, tree, or dog (or your idea of a teacher, tree, or dog), but your drawing is automatically copyrighted!

To get a copy of this activity, visit www.cherrylakepublishing.com/activities.

Anyone can braid their shoelaces. But a person needs special permission to use a photograph of braided shoelaces.

Once Grace's ideas are in a tangible format, could other people sell copies of her brochure? Turn in her brochure with their name on it as author? Make a CD or MP3 audio recording in which they read her writing out loud? Write and perform a play or TV show based on her video? Post her photograph on a Web page, wiki, or blog? The answer is no, unless Grace gives those people specific permission. In fact, if they try to put their name on Grace's work and claim they created it, it is **plagiarism**. This is stealing.

Copyright is a powerful idea and a powerful gift from countries to their citizen creators. It allows creators to be in charge of their work and to decide how it is used.

CHAPTER TWO

Public Domain, Trademarks, and Patents

This photo of a painting of George Washington is in the public domain, so you can use it freely. You can even alter it to fit your project's needs.

Another important part of copyright law is that copyright doesn't last forever. When copyright expires, the work is then considered part of the **public domain**. Public domain works "belong" to everyone to sell, change, mash up, mix up, and use to create new projects. Today, copyright expires 70 years after an author or a creator passes away. Also, any work created in the United States before 1923 is automatically in the public domain. It's a trade-off: the government protects the creator's work during his or her lifetime (and beyond). In exchange, the creator returns the work to the world afterward so that new work can be made from it. This allows us to create new things that build on earlier artists' creativity and expression. The materials created by people who work in the U.S. government is in the public domain, too. Some people even choose to give their works to the public domain right away. Together, we own a lot of public domain materials.

What Can You Read in the Public Domain?
Here are just a few examples:
- The Adventures of Sherlock Holmes by Arthur Conan Doyle
- Alice's Adventures in Wonderland by Lewis Carroll
- Peter Pan by J. M. Barrie
- The Tale of Peter Rabbit by Beatrix Potter

THE ADVENTURES OF SHERLOCK HOLMES
BY ARTHUR CONAN DOYLE

Logos such as Nike's Swoosh symbol are trademarked.

Remember how ideas cannot be copyrighted? There are other things that do not get copyright protection. For example, you cannot copyright basic facts, book titles, or fashion designs for clothing. Ingredient lists in recipes cannot be copyrighted, although illustrations or descriptions of the food and how to make it can be. Also, copyright is only one part of a larger set of protections and permissions called **intellectual property**. Intellectual property includes **trademarks** and **patents**. To protect their logos, companies can trademark them. The Nike swoosh and the McDonald's golden arches are registered trademarks. Inventions, which include drawings, blueprints, and descriptive writing, are protected by patents. Because there is a lot of competition over inventions, patents must be registered with the U.S. government.

TRY THIS!

Do these items fall under copyright protection?
1. A quote from the U.S. Constitution
2. A beautiful, hand-drawn map of Canada
3. A photograph of your pet
4. A photograph of your ancestor, taken in 1920
5. An X-ray of your broken arm
6. Beyoncé's newest hit
7. The book title Little House on the Prairie

ANSWERS:
1. No, public domain
2. Yes, because it is a work of art, not just the "facts" of where things are
3. Yes
4. No, because the photo was taken before 1923, so it is in the public domain
5. No, because an X-ray is considered a "fact"
6. Yes
7. No, because it is a book title

To get a copy of this activity, visit www.cherrylakepublishing.com/activities.

CHAPTER THREE
Sharing with Creative Commons

Creative Commons makes it easier to share information in today's fast-paced world.

Let's go back to the problem in the first chapter: needing to ask permission before using someone's copyrighted work. You make so many projects that are posted online or shared with others that it would be really inconvenient to ask for permission for every photo in every project, right? Life in the digital world moves much too fast for that, even though it is the right thing to do.

People can choose to give their photos a Creative Commons license so other people can use them easily.

What if there were a way for people to say up front, "I made this, I own the copyright, but you can use it if you want. Here's how you can use it without having to ask"?

There is! It's called Creative Commons, and many people have adopted it as a way of thinking about copyright and sharing. Creative Commons is an organization that has designed a system to show how a copyrighted work can be used. Its goal is to help people share their creative work in ways that make sense in today's digital world. It is a growing movement, and lots of organizations—from car manufacturers to major universities—are using it so materials are shared and reused more quickly. By using Creative Commons **licenses** (or CC licenses), creators allow

16

other people to share—legally—in the experience of making something new. We learn together, we share together.

Each creator decides how to license his or her work. Imagine that Maria has just taken a great photo of Mount Rushmore. She uses it in her report, and she thinks other kids might want to use it in theirs. What options does she have? One way is to do things the traditional way and require that people ask permission. Secondly, she could put her photo immediately into the public domain. Finally, she could hold on to her copyright but give it a Creative Commons license to encourage sharing. Creative Commons has designed six possible licenses. Each one can be abbreviated using the code words in parentheses.

Creative Commons was created to encourage sharing.

Creative Commons Attribution (CC BY)

http://creativecommons.org/licenses/by/3.0/

This is the most open license. It means that others can take Maria's photo and do whatever they want with it: sell it, crop it so we only see George Washington's face, draw a mustache on the faces, add words and turn it into a poster, or change it from color to black and white. However, they must give credit to Maria as the original photographer. This is what we mean by giving someone **attribution**.

Creative Commons Attribution-ShareAlike (CC BY-SA)

http://creativecommons.org/licenses/by-sa/3.0/

This license means that someone can do any of the things above. However, if someone uses Maria's CC BY-SA photo and adds his or her own words to make a poster, that person must give the poster a CC BY-SA license, too. So should someone who changes the colors in the photo or changes it in any other way.

Creative Commons Attribution-NonCommercial (CC BY-NC)

http://creativecommons.org/licenses/by-nc/3.0/

If Maria picks this license, other people can still use or change her photograph. But it must stay in the **noncommercial** world. This means that only Maria can make money from her photo. For example, Maria's teacher can use Maria's photo in a slideshow of national parks, as long as she gives credit to Maria. She can even share it with another teacher to use in his classroom. However, Maria's teacher could not sell copies of her slideshow. Then the teacher would have earned money from Maria's photo.

Creative Commons Attribution-NoDerivs (CC BY-ND)

http://creativecommons.org/licenses/by-nd/3.0/

Let's say that Maria loves her photograph exactly the way it is. She is happy to share it, but she doesn't want anybody cutting off part of her photo, changing the color, or adding a mustache. By picking this license, she tells people they are welcome to use her photo if they give her credit. But they cannot change it in any way or make any derivatives. They must reuse the original work as a whole.

Creative Commons Attribution-NonCommercial-ShareAlike

(CC BY-NC-SA)

http://creativecommons.org/licenses/by-nc-sa/3.0/

This is a combination of a few of the licenses above. If Maria licenses her photo this way, people have to give credit but cannot use it to make money. Additionally, whatever they create using Maria's photo must be licensed under the same license Maria chose: CC BY-NC-SA.

Creative Commons Attribution-NonCommercial-NoDerivs

(CC BY-NC-ND)

http://creativecommons.org/licenses/by-nc-nd/3.0/

This is the most limited license. People can use and share Maria's photo, but they can't change it. They also cannot make money from it.

The photographer who took this photo of Mount Rushmore chooses how other people are allowed to use it.

There are a lot of options for how to allow people to use a work. The same licenses would be used if, instead of a photo, Maria wanted to share her book, brochure, painting, music composition, song lyrics, podcast, or video. The licenses work for all kinds of creative work. There's even a tool to help you choose the license that is the best fit for you. Just visit *http://creativecommons.org/choose*.

But how do people know which license you've chosen? We'll talk about that next.

TRY THIS!

To get a copy of this activity, visit www.cherrylakepublishing.com/activities.

Which license would you choose for these works? Be sure to give reasons that support your choice.

1. You are part of a volunteer group that wants to remind kids to wear a bike helmet. You make a **public service announcement** and want people to spread the word everywhere.

2. You want to upload a scan of your favorite art project so other people can see it. You'd be happy if people used your scan on their Web sites or sold T-shirts with your photo on them.

3. Your friend's mom has written a seashell identification guide. She would love for seashell fans to use it and share it with each other. It would even be fun if somebody translated it so it could be used in another country. But she doesn't want someone to make money from her guide or their versions of it.

4. Your student council wrote an antibullying song. You hope that every school will adopt it and that some singers will record it. Getting people to learn the song is important, and you don't mind if some of the musicians make money from playing it.

5. Take a look at the back of this book's title page. Why do you think the publisher chose this Creative Commons license? What does it give you permission to do? What does it not give you permission to do?

22

CHAPTER FOUR

Choosing the License and Giving Credit

A user can add to or subtract from a Creative Commons photo that allows derivatives.

Earlier, Maria decided to share her Mount Rushmore photo and give people permission to use it. After talking with her parents, she chose a Creative Commons Attribution-ShareAlike (CC BY-SA) license. Maria isn't giving up her copyright by choosing a Creative

Commons license. The license just tells people what they can do with her copyrighted work.

Now Maria has to let people know that her work has been licensed. She can show someone she has added a CC license to her work in a few ways:

- Use the icon:
- Write out the full title of the license: Creative Commons Attribution-ShareAlike
- Use the abbreviation: CC BY-SA
- Select a CC license option when uploading the project to a sharing site like Flickr.com or YouTube.com

To use this image, give credit to the user. Use TASL (title-author-site-license) to describe it, like this: "U.S. Capitol, DC," by Francisco Diez on Flickr. This work is used under a Creative Commons Attribution 2.0 Generic License. http://creativecommons.org/licenses/by/2.0/deed.en

Not everybody knows Creative Commons as well as they know the © symbol for copyright. Because of this, the licensing label on your work should include a link back to the appropriate license page on the Creative Commons Web site (*http://creativecommons.org/licenses*). For example, for the CC BY-SA license above, you would link to *http://creativecommons.org/licenses/by-sa/3.0/*. This allows someone to read the license and understand what he or she can do with your work.

You can put the licensing information and link on the title page or an attributions page at the end of a presentation or report. You can add it to video credits or make a note in the corner of a photograph. Just make sure a reader or viewer can find the Uniform Resource Locator (URL), or Web address. Including the word *copyright* and the date a work was created is a good habit. It reminds others that your work is still yours. The Creative Commons license just explains how you are sharing your rights as a copyright holder.

Are you curious about what kinds of works have a CC license? Try the Creative Commons search tool at http://search.creativecommons.org. Can you find the things listed below by searching there? What Creative Commons license did the creator choose for each example?

To get a copy of this activity, visit www.cherrylakepublishing.com/activities.

1. Photo of a dog
2. Recording of "Moonlight Sonata" by the composer Ludwig van Beethoven
3. Piece of clip art of a computer
4. Video about otters on YouTube

If Jeremy crops and uses Maria's photo in his History Day poster, he needs to show that he has used her photo. He can use the memory clue TASL (said like "tassel") to remember how to give her credit: Title of the work, Author (or creator), Source (where he found it), and License. Here is an example:

"Mount Rushmore" photo by Maria Fuente on Flickr .com. Used with a Creative Commons BY-SA license. (http://creativecommons.org/licenses/by-sa/3.0/)

If you make something on the computer that won't get printed out, you can also include a link to the license for others to read. Like this:

Emily Puckett Rodgers. Copyright 2013. This work is licensed under a Creative Commons-Attribution 3.0 license (http://creativecommons.org/licenses/by/3.0/).

CHAPTER FIVE

Finding Creative Commons Materials for Your Class Projects

There are many online tools to help you find Creative Commons materials.

Now you know how to find out if a work is licensed under Creative Commons. But where can you go to find great Creative Commons images, audio recordings, videos, and text? Actually, it's easy, and there are millions of materials that have been licensed for this purpose!

One great place to start is Creative Commons Search page, *http://search.creativecommons.org*. It will search numerous libraries of CC content. These libraries include Google Images for photos and drawings, YouTube for videos, Jamendo for music, and Wikimedia Commons for all types of media. You can also use the advanced search feature of Google.com. Start a search, then click on the gear in the right-hand corner of the screen to choose advanced settings. For CC images, *http://FlickrCC.bluemountains.net* and *http://TheNounProject.com* have easy search options.

The Noun Project makes simple icons such as these freely available to the public.

TRY THIS!

Write a short story and have a friend do the same. Then trade stories. Find an image to accompany your friend's story using the Creative Commons search page, the Noun Project (http://thenounproject.com), the Flickr Creative Commons search (www.flickr.com/creativecommons), the Flickr.cc search tool (http://flickrcc. bluemountains.net), or a Google Images advanced search (http://images.google.com; click on the gear after you start your search to get to advanced settings). Remember to add the image's attribution either right below the image or on a special attributions page at the end of the story.

To get a copy of this activity, visit www.cherrylakepublishing.com/activities.

While these search tools do a great job, you also need to check the license for whatever you find. Make sure you understand how you can use the image or other material.

You know how to search, use, and license Creative Commons content. You're now part of the community of creators who share and build on each other's work. Welcome!

Glossary

attribution (a-truh-BYOO-shuhn) a note giving credit to another source or work

copyrighted (KAH-pee-rite-id) legally controlled by an author, artist, or other creator

derivatives (duh-RIV-uh-tivz) something taken from or based on another work

intellectual property (in-tuh-LEK-choo-uhl PRAH-pur-tee) creative works that are legally protected by copyright, trademark, or patent

licenses (LYE-suhns-ez) documents that officially grant permission for a person to own, use, or do something

noncommerical (non-kuh-MUR-shul) not for profit

patents (PAT-uhnts) legal documents giving the inventor of an item the sole rights to manufacture or sell it

plagiarism (PLAY-jur-iz-um) the act of stealing the ideas or words of another person and presenting them as one's own

public domain (PUHB-lik doh-MANE) work that is unprotected by copyright and is therefore available to everyone to use or copy

public service announcement (PUHB-lik SUR-viss uh-NOUNS-muhnt) a commercial that encourages people to take action for health, safety, or the good of the community

tangible format (TAN-jih-bul FOR-mat) works that can be seen, touched, heard, or otherwise experienced, and therefore can be copyrighted

trademarks (TRADE-mahrks) words, pictures, or designs that show that a product is made by a particular company

Find Out More

BOOKS

Aoki, Keith, James Boyle, and Jennifer Jenkins. *Bound by Law? Tales from the Public Domain*. Durham, NC: Duke University Press, 2008. (Available in print or as a free digital download at *http://web.law.duke.edu/cspd/comics/*)

Creative Commons. *The Power of Open*. e-book retrieved August 18, 2012, from *http://thepowerofopen.org*.

Popek, Emily. *Copyright and Digital Ethics*. New York: Rosen Central, 2011.

WEB SITES

Creative Commons

http://creativecommons.org

Learn about the Creative Commons organization and the six CC licenses; search for CC images, video, and audio you can use in your projects; and use the online tool to help you figure out which CC license is right for your work.

Teaching Copyright

www.teachingcopyright.org

This is a set of lesson plans to help teens learn about copyright in the digital age.

Index

About the Authors

Emily Puckett Rodgers helps faculty, students, and staff at the University of Michigan share their educational resources with the global learning community.

Kristin Fontichiaro teaches at the University of Michigan. She has written many books for students and adults.

Index

Internet Sites

FactHound offers a safe, fun way to find Internet sites related to this book. All of the sites on FactHound have been researched by our staff.

Here's how:
1. Visit *www.facthound.com*
2. Type in this special code **073682457X** for age-appropriate sites. Or enter a search word related to this book for a more general search.
3. Click on the **Fetch It** button.

FactHound will fetch the best sites for you!